Iran

2012 International Religi

United States Department of State,

Bureau of Democracy, Human Rights and Labor

Table of Contents

Executive Summary 1

Section I. Religious Demography 6

Section II. Status of Government Respect for Religious Freedom, Legal Policy and Framework...........................8

Section II. Status of Government Respect for Religious Freedom, Government Practices..19

Section III. Status of Societal Respect for Religious Freedom..46

Section IV. U.S. Government Policy 50

Executive Summary

The constitution and other laws and policies do not protect religious freedom, and in practice, the government severely restricted religious freedom. The government's respect for religious freedom declined during the year. There were increased reports of the government charging religious and ethnic minorities with moharebeh (enmity against God), "anti-Islamic propaganda," or vague national security crimes for their religious activities. Those reportedly arrested on religious grounds faced worsening prison conditions and treatment, as with most prisoners of conscience. The arrest and harassment of members of religious minorities also increased significantly during the year. There continued to be reports of the government imprisoning, harassing, intimidating, and discriminating against people because of their religious beliefs. The constitution states that Ja'afari (Twelver) Shia Islam is the official state religion. It provides that "other Islamic denominations are to be accorded full respect" and officially recognizes only three non-Islamic religious groups, Zoroastrians, Christians, and Jews, as religious minorities. Although the constitution protects the rights of members of these three religions to practice freely, the government imposed legal restrictions on proselytizing and regularly arrests members of the Zoroastrian and Christian communities for practicing their religion. The government regularly vilified Judaism. The government considers Bahais to be apostates and defines the Bahai Faith as a "political sect." The government prohibits Bahais from teaching and practicing their faith and subjects them to many forms of discrimination not faced by members of other religious groups.

Government rhetoric and actions created a threatening atmosphere for nearly all non-Shia religious groups, most notably for Bahais, as well as for Sufi Muslims, evangelical Christians, Jews, and

Shia groups not sharing the government's official religious views. Bahai and Christian groups reported arbitrary arrests, prolonged detentions, and confiscation of property. Government-controlled broadcast and print media continued negative campaigns against religious minorities, particularly Bahais. All religious minorities suffered varying degrees of officially sanctioned discrimination, particularly in the areas of employment, education, and housing. Bahais continued to experience expulsions from, or denial of admission to, universities.

There were reports of societal abuses and discrimination based on religious affiliation, belief, or practice. Members of non-Shia religious groups faced some societal discrimination, and elements of society created a threatening atmosphere for some religious minorities. However, reports indicated the government was the primary instigator of the abuse of religious freedom. The government's campaign against non-Shias created an atmosphere of impunity allowing other elements of society to harass religious minorities.

Since 1999 the United States has designated Iran as a "Country of Particular Concern" (CPC) under the International Religious Freedom Act. In 2011 the secretary of state redesignated Iran as a CPC, and redesignated the existing restrictions on certain imports from and exports to Iran. The U.S. government made clear its strong objections to the Iranian government's harsh and oppressive treatment of religious minorities and pushed for improvements in the country through high-level public statements and reports, support for relevant United Nations (UN) and nongovernmental organization (NGO) efforts, coordinated diplomatic initiatives with the international community, and sanctions. The U.S. government also engaged with NGOs and civil society to gain a greater understanding of the status of religious freedom in the country. The United States has no diplomatic relations with Iran.

Section I. Religious Demography

According to the Statistical Center of Iran's 2011 National Population and Housing Census, the population is 75.2 million. Muslims constitute 99 percent of the population; 90 percent are Shia and 9 percent are Sunni (mostly Turkmen, Arabs, Baluchs, and Kurds living in the southwest, southeast, and northwest, respectively). There are no official statistics available on the size of the Sufi Muslim population; however, some reports estimate between two and five million people practice Sufism.

Groups together constituting the remaining 1 percent of the population include Bahais, Christians, Jews, Sabean-Mandaeans, and Zoroastrians. The two largest non-Muslim minorities are Bahais and Christians. The Bahais number approximately 300,000, and are heavily concentrated in Tehran and Semnan. According to UN figures, 300,000 Christians live in the country, though some NGOs estimate there may be as many as 370,000. The Statistical Center of

Iran reports there are 117,700. The majority of Christians are ethnic Armenians concentrated in Tehran and Isfahan. Unofficial estimates of the Assyrian Christian population range between 10,000 and 20,000. There are also Protestant denominations, including evangelical groups. Christian groups outside the country estimate the size of the Protestant Christian community to be less than 10,000, although many Protestant Christians reportedly practice in secret. There are from 5,000 to 10,000 Sabean-Mandaeans. The Statistical Center of Iran estimates there are 25,271 Zoroastrians, who are primarily ethnic Persians; however, Zoroastrian groups report they have 60,000 members.

Section II. Status of Government Respect for Religious Freedom

Legal/Policy Framework

The constitution and other laws and policies severely restrict freedom of religion. The constitution declares the "official religion is Islam and the doctrine followed is that of Ja'afari (Twelver) Shiism." The constitution states all laws and regulations must be based on undefined "Islamic criteria" and official interpretation of Sharia (Islamic law).

The constitution provides Sunni Muslims a degree of religious freedom, and states that, "within the limits of the law," Zoroastrians, Jews, and Christians are the only recognized religious minorities with protected freedom to worship freely and to form religious societies, as long as they do not proselytize. Although the Sabean-Mandaeans do not consider themselves Christians, the government regards them as Christians, and thus they are included among the three recognized religious minorities. The government does not recognize any other non-Islamic religion, and adherents of these other religious groups, such as the Bahais, do not have the freedom to practice their beliefs.

Supreme Leader of the Islamic Revolution Ayatollah Ali Khamenei heads a three-branch government structure (legislative, executive, and judicial branches). A group of 86 Islamic scholars known as the Assembly of Experts chooses the supreme leader. The scholars are directly elected every eight years. The unelected Council of Guardians reviews all acts of the Majlis (parliament) for strict conformity with Islamic law and the constitution, and all candidates for any elected office, including the Assembly of Experts. The council is composed of six clerics appointed by the supreme leader and six Muslim legal scholars nominated by the judiciary and approved by the Majlis.

The constitution does not provide for the rights of Muslim citizens to choose, change, or renounce their religious beliefs. The government automatically considers a child born to a Muslim father to be a Muslim and deems conversion from Islam to be apostasy, which is punishable by death.

Non-Muslims may not engage in public religious expression, persuasion, or conversion among Muslims. Such proselytizing is punishable by death. The government restricts published religious material. Government officials frequently confiscate Christian Bibles and pressure publishing houses printing Bibles or non-sanctioned non-Muslim materials to cease operations.

The Ministry of Culture and Islamic Guidance (Ershad) and the Ministry of Intelligence and Security closely monitor religious activity. The government does not require members of some recognized religious minorities to register, but the authorities closely monitor their communal, religious, and cultural events and organizations, including schools. The government requires evangelical Christian congregations to compile and submit membership lists. The government requires Bahais to register with the police.

Non-Muslim religious minorities may not be elected to a representative body or hold senior government or military positions, with the exception of five of the 290 Majlis seats reserved by the government for religious minorities. There are two seats for Armenian Christians, one for Assyrian Christians, one for Jews, and one for Zoroastrians. Sunnis do not have reserved seats in the Majlis but are permitted to serve in the body. Sunni Majlis deputies tend to be elected from among the larger Sunni communities. The government allows religious minorities to vote; however, religious minorities, including Sunni Muslims, are ineligible to be president.

Members of religious minority groups, except Sunni Muslims, may not serve in the judiciary, security services, or as public school principals. Officials screen applicants for public sector employment for their adherence to and knowledge of Islam, although members of religious minorities, with the exception of Bahais, may serve in lower ranks of government. Government workers who do not observe Islamic principles and rules are subject to penalties. Bahais are barred from all leadership positions in the government and military.

The constitution states the army must be Islamic, in the sense that it must be committed to Islamic ideals and must recruit individuals who are committed to the objectives of the Islamic Revolution. In practice, however, no members of religious minority groups are exempt from military service. The law forbids non-Muslims from holding officer positions over Muslims in the armed forces. Members of constitutionally protected religious minorities with a college education may serve as officers during their mandatory military service but may not be career military officers.

Article 297 of the amended 1991 Islamic Punishments Act authorizes collection of equal diyeh (blood money) as restitution to families for the death of both Muslims and non-Muslims. According to law, Bahai blood is considered "mobah," meaning it can be spilled with impunity and Bahai families are not entitled to restitution.

The government generally allows recognized religious minority groups to open schools. The Ministry of Education imposes certain curriculum requirements and supervises these schools. With few exceptions, the directors of such private schools must be Muslim. Members of recognized religious minority groups are not required to attend these schools. The Ministry of Education must approve all textbooks used in coursework, including religious texts. Members of recognized religious minority groups may provide religious instruction in non-Persian languages, but authorities must approve their texts. This requirement sometimes imposes significant translation expenses on minority communities.

The government, since the Islamic Revolution, formally denies Bahai students access to higher education. In 1991 the Supreme Council of the Cultural Revolution signed a secret memorandum stating that Bahais "must be expelled from universities" and that Bahai children "should be enrolled in schools which have a strong and imposing religious ideology," presumably to indoctrinate Bahais in a state-supported religion. The Ministry of Justice states Bahais are permitted to enroll in schools only if they do not identify themselves as such. To register for the university entrance examination the government requires Bahai students to identify themselves as a religion other than Bahai. These requirements preclude Bahai enrollment in state-run universities, because a tenet of the Bahai faith is not to deny one's faith. The Ministry of Justice requires universities to exclude Bahais or expel them if their religious affiliation becomes known. University applicants are required to pass an examination in Islamic, Christian, or Jewish theology, but there is no test for Bahai theology.

Non-Shia religious leaders report bans on Sunni religious literature and on Sunni teachings in public schools. Sunnis may not build new schools or mosques.

Bahais are banned from the social pension system. In addition, Bahais are regularly denied compensation for injury or criminal victimization and the right to inherit property. The government does not recognize Bahai marriages and divorces but allows a civil attestation of marriage to serve as a marriage certificate.

The government allows recognized religious minority groups to establish community centers and certain self-financed cultural, social, athletic, or charitable associations. However, the government prohibits the Bahai community from officially assembling or maintaining administrative institutions and actively closes such institutions as part of this policy.

Jewish citizens are free to travel out of the country, and the government generally does not enforce legal restrictions on travel to Israel by Jewish citizens. Other citizens may not travel to Israel.

The government carefully monitors the statements and views of senior Shia religious leaders. The constitution does not provide for the Special Clerical Courts, established to investigate offenses and crimes committed by clerics. The supreme leader oversees these courts, which operate outside the judiciary.

The government maintains a legal interpretation of Islam that effectively deprives women of many rights granted to men. The government enforces gender segregation throughout the country without regard to religious affiliation. Women of all religious groups are expected to adhere to "Islamic dress" in public; this includes covering their hair and fully covering the body in loose clothing. Although enforcement of rules for such conservative dress eases at times, the government periodically punishes "un-Islamic dress." The government's 12-point template contract for marriage and divorce, while not mandatory, limits the rights accorded to all women by custom and traditional interpretations of Islamic law.

The government observes the following religious holidays as national holidays: Eid-e-Ghadir, Tassoua, Ashura, Arbaeen, the Demise of the Prophet Muhammad, Martyrdom of Imam Reza, Birthday of Imam Ali, Ascension of the Prophet Muhammad,

Birthday of Imam Mahdi, Eid-e-Fitr (Eid al-Fitr), Martyrdom of Imam Ali, Martyrdom of Imam Jafar Sadegh, Eid-e-Ghorban (Eid al-Adha), and the Islamic New Year.

Section II. Status of Government Respect for Religious Freedom

Government Practices

There were reports of abuses of religious freedom, including imprisonment and detention. The government severely restricted religious freedom. Reports of government imprisonment, harassment, intimidation, and discrimination based on religious beliefs continued. Government rhetoric and actions created an increasingly threatening atmosphere for nearly all non-Shia religious groups, most notably for Bahais, as well as for Sunni Muslims including Sufis, evangelical Christians, Jews, and Shia groups that did not share the government's religious views. Government-controlled broadcast and print media continued negative campaigns against religious minorities, particularly against Bahais. All non-Shia religious minorities suffered varying degrees of officially sanctioned discrimination, especially in employment, education, and housing.

The government continued to increase convictions and executions of dissidents, political reformists, and peaceful protesters on the charge of moharebeh (enmity against God) and anti-Islamic propaganda. The government executed at least ten individuals on charges of moharebeh, according to credible NGO reports. In June authorities executed four ethnic Arabs from the Ahvaz region who had been arrested in April 2011 during a protest in Khuzestan and convicted of moharebeh and fasad-fil arz ("corruption on earth"). The authorities reportedly executed at least six Salafi Kurds on December 27 on charges of "membership in Salafi groups" and "participation in terrorist acts."

Christian pastor Youcef Nadarkhani remained in jail at year's end, after a series of government actions including a brief release from imprisonment. In September, he was acquitted of 2010 charges of apostasy, which carried a death sentence, but convicted of evangelizing Muslims, given a three-year sentence, and released with time served. Authorities re-arrested Nadarkhani on December 22 to serve 45 days remaining from the three-year sentence. Officials reportedly pressured Nadarkhani to renounce his Christian faith throughout his ordeal and offered leniency if he would do so. In March the authorities briefly detained Nadarkhani's lawyer and prominent human rights attorney, Mohammed Ali Dadkhah, who was convicted in July 2011 of "propaganda against the regime." Dadkhah reported to Evin Prison in September, shortly after Nadarkhani's initial release, to begin serving a nine-year sentence.

Christian pastor and dual U.S.-Iranian national, Saeed Abedini, was put under house arrest in July on charges of undermining national security by leading a network of house churches. In September, Islamic Revolutionary Guard Corps officials raided his residence and took him to Evin Prison, where he remained in detention at year's end. Abedini was reportedly subjected to physical and psychological abuse by Iranian authorities. Iranian officials have denied him consular access and necessary medical care.

In September Ayatollah Hassan Sanei, head of a state-run charity trust, raised the reward for killing Salman Rushdi by 6 billion Iranian rials ($500,000) to 40.5 billion IRR ($3.3 million). Rushdi has been the target of a fatwa on charges of blasphemy since 1989.

Since the 1979 Islamic Revolution, the government has executed more than 200 Bahais, although there were no reports of Bahai executions during the year. The government frequently prevented many Bahais from leaving the country, harassed and persecuted them, and generally disregarded their property rights.

The government arrested at least 60 Bahais arbitrarily during the year, and released some. At year's end, at least 116 Bahais were in detention and 524 Bahai cases were still active in the judicial system, according to human rights groups. In many cases the government charged them with violating Islamic penal code articles 500 and 698, relating to activities against the state and spreading falsehoods, respectively. The government also often charged Bahais with "espionage on behalf of Zionism," partly because Bahai world headquarters is located in Israel. These charges were more acute when the government found that Bahais were communicating with or sending monetary contributions to the Bahai headquarters. Often the charges were not dropped upon release, and those with charges pending against them reportedly feared arrest at any time. Most were released only after paying a large fine or posting high bail. For some, bail was in the form of deeds of property. Others gained release in exchange for personal guarantees from a "guardian" that the offender would appear in court, or from depositing a work license as a surety to appear when summoned to court or prison. Government officials reportedly offered Bahais relief from mistreatment in exchange for recanting their religious affiliation. It required incarcerated Bahais to recant their religious affiliation as a precondition for release.

Seven Bahai leaders (Fariba Kamalabadi, Jamaloddin Khanjani, Afif Naeimi, Behrouz Tavakkoli, Saeid Rezaie, Vahid Tizfahm, and Mahvash Sabet) remained in detention at year's end, serving sentences extended by the authorities in 2011 to 20 years. They were charged in 2011 with "espionage for Israel, insulting religious sancities, and propaganda against the Islamic Republic." The government did not allow any of the seven access to their attorney, Abdolfattah Soltani, who was arrested in September 2011 on charges including "spreading propaganda against the system," "setting up an illegal opposition group," and "gathering and colluding with intent to harm national security." In March the authorities sentenced Soltani to 18 years in prison and banned him for an additional 20 years from practicing law. His wife and imprisoned lawyer, Massoumeh Dehghan, was charged with spreading propaganda against the state, sentenced in November to one year in prison, and banned from leaving the country.

In February the authorities sentenced Adel Fanaian, a member of the Bahai faith, to six years in prison on charges of "mobilizing a group with the intent to disturb national security" and "propaganda against the regime." He was first arrested in 2010 and released on bail. At least six other Bahais (Pouya Tebyanian, Faramarz Firouzian, Anisa Ighani, Taraneh Torabi, Jinous Nurani, and Rufia Bidaghi) were sentenced during the year on similar charges to terms ranging from one to six and a half years. Firouzian, Ighani, Nurani, Tebyanian, and Bidaghi remained in prison at year's end.

The chief prosecutor of Tehran announced the intelligence authorities arrested 28 Iranians in Tehran in December for being in close contact with foreign-based television networks that advocate the Bahai faith. Authorities did not release the names of those arrested or the specific charges against them.

The government raided Bahai homes and businesses and confiscated large amounts of private and commercial property, as well as religious materials. The government also seized private homes in which Bahai youth classes were held, despite the fact that the owners had proper ownership documents. The government continued to hold many Bahai properties it seized following the 1979 revolution, including cemeteries, holy places, historical sites, and administrative centers. The government generally prevented Bahais from burying their dead in accordance with their religious tradition, and many of their cemeteries were destroyed in previous years.

There were reports of authorities forcing Bahai businesses to close, placing restrictions on their businesses, asking managers of private companies to dismiss Bahai employees, and denying applications for new or renewed business and trade licenses. In May officials from the Ministry of Intelligence and Security reportedly raided two factories owned fully or partially by Bahais in Semnan, sealed the facilities and shut down operations.

The Association of Chambers of Commerce (a nominally independent organization heavily influenced by the government) reportedly began compiling a list of Bahais as well as their trades and employment. It also instructed trade associations and unions to collect the same information. Once identified, Bahai businesses were reportedly closed, business licenses or leases were rejected or not renewed, and non-Bahai businesses were instructed not to engage with Bahai-owned companies.

Although the government maintained publicly that Bahais were free to attend university if they did not identify themselves as Bahai, public and private universities continued to deny admittance and expel Bahai students, indicating the implicit policy of preventing Bahais from obtaining higher education remained in effect. After their arrest for "membership in the Bahai community" in 2011, Fuad Moqaddam and Emanullah Mostaqim of the Bahai Institute for Higher Education were both sentenced in 2012 to five-year prison terms. Mostaqim was reportedly free on bail at year's end. Moqaddam's status was unknown.

The Bahai Institute for Higher Education, established in 1987, reportedly was declared illegal in 2011 based on undefined "national security concerns." The government continued to imprison and detain members of the Bahai Institute for Higher Education throughout the year. Professors Kamran Rahimian, Faran Hesami, Keyvan Rahimian, and Shakib Nasrollah were found guilty in 2011 on charges of "membership in the Bahai community" and "gathering and colluding to disturb national security." Kamran Rahimian was sentenced to four years in prison in January and was serving his sentence at year's end. Kamran's wife, Hesami, was also sentenced in January and began serving her four-year sentence in July. Keyvan was sentenced to five years in jail in June and began serving his sentence in September. No further information was available on Nasrollah's case, but he was believed to be in prison at year's end. The Bahai defendants were unable to consult their lawyer, Abdolfattah Soltani, who was also detained in 2011.

The government's on-going seizure of Bahai personal property and its denial of access to education and employment eroded the Bahai community's economic base and threatened its survival. Members of the Bahai community reported Bahai children in public schools faced attempts by their teachers and administrators to convert them to Islam. The detention of Bahai students continued during the year. Two female students, Leva Khanjani and Nasim Sultan Beigi, were reportedly detained in Tehran and sent to Evin Prison in August. Leva Khanjani was sentenced to two years in prison on charges relating to her participation in the December 2009 post-election student protests.

Harassment and arrests of Sufis also continued during the year. Seventeen Gonabadi dervishes from Kavar, previously acquitted of charges of "enmity against God" and "corruption on earth," were summoned again in July to the Revolutionary Court in Shiraz on charges of "acting against national security," "disturbing public order," "assault and battery," and carrying illegal weapons. In September Nosrat Tabasi began serving a six-month prison term after being sentenced to five years in prison with four and a half years suspended; Ali Reza Roshan was sentenced to a year in prison and four years suspended sentence on charges of "gathering and colluding to disturb national security." The government still held approximately 15 Sufi Web masters and journalists arrested in September 2011. Several Sufi prisoners reportedly suffered from malnutrition and a lack of medical care.

Security forces arrested or detained members of Maktabe Quran, a Kurdish Sunni group. Abdullah Abbasi, a leading figure in the office of Hasan Amini, head of the Maktabe Quran, was reportedly detained in August on unspecified charges and remained in prison at year's end. In November three other members were summoned and interrogated about the group's activities. In September the Ministry of Education banned 17 teachers, who are reported to be members of the group, from teaching in Kurdish towns. Shaikh Hussein-Panahi, the head of Shar'ee public judge's office in Kurdistan, was arrested in September on unspecified charges. There were also reports that several members of the Sunni community were summoned to the security bureaus for questioning.

The authorities reportedly arrested several hundred Christians, including members of evangelical groups. The status of many of these cases was not known at year's end. Authorities released some Christians almost immediately, but held others in secret locations without access to attorneys. Authorities also arrested several members of "protected" Christian groups such as Armenian Apostolics and Assyrians. Prison authorities reportedly withheld proper medical care from such prisoners, according to human rights groups. In one such case, Pastor Behnam Irani suffered in prison from a blood infection without medical attention.

In September authorities reportedly raided four house churches in Fars province and arrested forty Christians on suspicion of "having contact with the enemies of the Islamic regime abroad" and "holding Christian services at their homes." The status of these cases was unclear at year's end. According to NGO reports, some were freed following payment of significant bail fees; the Intelligence Ministry allegedly continued to hold at least 10 individuals.

In October the authorities sentenced Pastor Farhad Sabokrouh, Shahnaz Jazan, Davood (David) Ali-Jani, and Naser Zamen-Dezfuli, four Christians arrested in December 2011, to one year in prison on charges of "missionary activities and anti-regime propaganda through spreading of Christianity." Their sentences were suspended pending appeal.

Security forces raided Christmas celebrations, arresting 50 Christian converts in a December 27 raid in Tehran and interrogating them for hours before their release. Armenian Christian pastor Vruir Avenessian was also arrested during the raid.

Muslim converts to Christianity faced harassment, arrest, and sentencing. Many arrests took place during police raids on religious gatherings, when the government also confiscated religious property. Ten Christian converts were arrested in February in Shiraz at a residence used as a church. In October security forces raided the homes of four Christian converts (Shahab Samimi, Fariba Karimkhani, Farshad Rahimdel, and Yasser Mirza Zanjani), confiscated some of their property, and arrested them, allegedly due to their religious activities.

Zoroastrians also reported detentions and harassment. There was no information on the whereabouts or trial of Yashin Jamshidi, a Zoroastrian in Karaj, whom Ministry of Intelligence agents arrested in October 2011.

There were reports of arrests and harassment of Sunnis. Molavi Fathi Naghshbandi, a Sunni leader in the city of Rask, was arrested with several Sunni scholars in April in connection with the assassination of pro-government Sunni cleric Molavi Mostafa Jang Zehi in January. The arrest of his son Abdolghafar Naghshbandi in May inflamed protests, upon which authorities reportedly opened fire, killing at least one person.

Shia religious leaders who did not fully support government policies or the supreme leader's views also faced intimidation and arrest. Prison conditions remained poor for dissident Shia cleric Ayatollah Hossein Kazemeini Boroujerdi, who was serving an 11-year sentence on unspecified charges in Evin Prison and suffering from several health problems. In March inmates allegedly poisoned his food. His supporters and family were also reportedly harassed and attacked. For example, in October, a close relative, Fatemeh Sameni, was injured after a driver reportedly struck her with his car. Another unidentified driver similarly assaulted her earlier in the year.

In August Dr. Kamran Ayazi was flogged and suffered severe bleeding after being convicted of criticizing Islam on Internet message boards. He is currently serving a nine-year sentence on charges of "enmity against God."

There were reports of increased enforcement of dress codes; those arrested were subject to fines or other punishment, including whipping. Ahmad Rouzbehani, head of the "morality police," stated in

May that "70,000 police officers are being deployed to confront dress code violations on the street." There were reports in June that an actress was arrested for "inappropriate hijab" when she was en route to a concert in Tehran. A number of women attending the same event were also reportedly arrested on the same charges.

The government actively denied Christians freedom of religion. Christians, particularly evangelicals, experienced increased harassment and surveillance during the year.

The government enforced prohibition on proselytizing by closely monitoring the activities of evangelical Christians, discouraging Muslims from entering church premises, closing churches, and arresting Christian converts. Authorities pressed evangelical church leaders to sign pledges that they would not evangelize Muslims or allow Muslims to attend church services. Meetings for evangelical services are restricted to Sundays. Reports suggested authorities regarded the act of allowing Muslims to visit a Christian church as proselytizing. Members of evangelical congregations were required to carry membership cards, photocopies of which had to be provided to the authorities. Authorities posted outside congregation centers subjected worshippers to identity checks.

The International Campaign for Human Rights, an NGO, reported the Islamic Revolutionary Guard Corps gained oversight of churches, replacing the Ministry of Intelligence and Ministry of Culture and Islamic Guidance. Christians of all denominations reported the presence of security cameras outside their churches, allegedly to confirm that no non-Christians participated in services.

Cyber police units raided the houses and confiscated the properties of some Christians. For example, they raided blogger and Christian convert Alireza Ebrahimi's home in November. Ebrahimi was not at the house and his whereabouts were unknown at year's end. The police in November also arrested two other Christian converts, Saeed Mirzaei and Sadegh Mirzaei, on charges of "propagating against Islam" and "action against national security."

Official reports and the media continued to characterize Christian house churches as "illegal networks" and "Zionist propaganda institutions." Arrested members of house churches were often accused of being supported by enemy countries. In May five members of a house church were detained in Shiraz for, among other charges, "propagation against the Islamic regime" and "defaming Islamic holy figures through Christian evangelizing." They were in prison awaiting trial at year's end.

Assyrian Christians reported their community was permitted to write its own textbooks which, following government authorization, were printed at the government's expense and distributed to the Assyrian community. The government reportedly allowed Hebrew instruction but limited the distribution of Hebrew texts, particularly nonreligious texts, making it difficult to teach the language. The government required Jewish schools to remain open on Saturdays, a violation of Jewish religious law, to conform to the schedule of other schools.

With some exceptions, there was little government restriction of, or interference with, Jewish religious practice. However, the Jewish community experienced official discrimination. Government officials continued to make anti-Semitic statements, organize events designed to deny the Holocaust, and sanction anti-Semitic propaganda. Such propaganda involved official statements, media outlets, publications, and books. The government's anti-Semitic rhetoric, as well as the perception among radical Muslims that all Jewish citizens of the country supported Zionism and the state of Israel, continued to create a hostile atmosphere for Jews. The rhetorical attacks also further blurred the lines between

Zionism, Judaism, and Israel, and contributed to increased concerns about the future security of the Jewish community in the country. In an August statement, President Ahmadinejad conflated Zionists with Jews when he stated, "It has now been some 400 years that a horrendous Zionist clan has been ruling the major world affairs, and behind the scenes of the major power circles, in political, media, monetary, and banking organizations in the world." Supreme Leader Ayatollah Khamenei made similar statements in an August speech referring to the Zionist regime and Zionists as a "cancerous tumor."

Ahmadinejad continued to question the existence and the scope of the Holocaust and publicly called for the destruction of Israel. His rhetoric combined with that of the supreme leader created a more hostile environment for the Jewish community. In his interview with French journalists on September 9 he stated, "The Zionist regime relies on the Holocaust and if it is taken away from the regime, the philosophy of its existence disappears and all politics in the international arena which were based on it will come undone."

The Iranian Documentary and Experimental Film Center produced a film called "The Anti-Semite" or "Yahod Setiz," which makes a mockery of the Nazi concentration camp Auschwitz. On May 25, the Cannes Film Festival decided to drop this film from its program, describing it as offensive.

In late June, during an international antidrug conference in Tehran, Vice President Mohammad-Reza Rahimi gave an anti-Semitic speech blaming the "Zionists" for spreading illegal drugs around the world, using as proof that not a single Zionist is a drug addict. Iran News later reported that Rahimi's office denied he made anti-Semitic and racist remarks.

Authorities also harassed and repressed the Sabean-Mandaean religious community in ways similar to its harassment of other minority religious groups, including often denying members of the Sabean-Mandaean community access to higher education.

There were reports of arrests and harassment of Sunni clerics and congregants. Many Sunnis claimed they were discriminated against; however, it was difficult to distinguish whether the cause of discrimination was religious or ethnic, since most Sunnis are also members of ethnic minorities. Sunnis cited the absence of a Sunni mosque in Tehran, despite the presence of more than one million Sunnis in the city, as a prominent example. Sunni leaders reported bans on Sunni religious literature and teachings in public schools, even in predominantly Sunni areas. Sunnis also noted the underrepresentation of Sunnis in government-appointed positions in the provinces where they form a majority, such as Kurdistan and Khuzestan, as well as their inability to obtain senior government positions. Residents of provinces with large Sunni populations, including Kurdistan, Khuzestan, and Sistan-va-Baluchestan, reported discrimination, lack of basic government services, and adequate funding for infrastructure projects.

In December 2011 Sunni members of the Majlis sent a letter to the supreme leader asking for the implementation of the constitutional principles on religious freedom, permission to build a mosque in Tehran, and the right to run in presidential elections. No official response was reported by year's end.

Security officials continued to raid prayer sites belonging to Sunnis and prevented them from holding religious ceremonies marking the Feast of the Sacrifice (Eid al-Adha). There were reports from NGOs that 19 Sunni Arabs were arrested in Khuzestan before the religious holiday of Eid Al-Fitr. Sunnis in Tehran were prevented from entering houses they rented for religious ceremonies. They were also required to have a Shia imam lead their prayers.

The government repressed Sufi communities and their religious practices. Intelligence and security services increased their harassment and intimidation of prominent Sufi leaders. Government restrictions on Sufi groups and husseiniya (houses of worship) have become more pronounced in recent years. Government officials destroyed Sufi homes, businesses, and religious sites during the year.

The government reportedly used the clerical courts to prosecute certain clerics for expressing controversial political ideas and for participating in nonreligious activities, including journalism. In February agents of the special clerical court sealed the door to the library of the late dissident cleric Ayatollah Hossein Ali Montazeri, as well as the door to the residence of his son, Ahmad. In July NGOs reported that dissident cleric and blogger Arash Honarvar Shojaee, convicted in 2010 on espionage charges, would face a new trial in the Special Clerical Court for "publishing falsehoods with the intent to create public anxiety." There was no update on his trial status at year's end.

Dr. Ahmed Shaheed, UN Special Rapporteur for Human Rights in Iran, submitted his third report in September, in which he noted "members of both recognized and unrecognized religions have reported various levels of intimidation, arrest, detention, and interrogation that focus on their religious beliefs." He also stated "the reports and interviews continue to portray a disturbing trend with regard to religious freedom in the country."

Section III. Status of Societal Respect for Religious Freedom

There were reports of societal abuses or discrimination based on religious affiliation, belief, or practice. Although the constitution gave Christians, Jews, and Zoroastrians the status of "protected" religious minorities, in practice non-Muslims faced substantial societal discrimination, and government actions continued to support elements of society that created a threatening atmosphere for them. Many reports from human rights organizations and international organizations during the year asserted that societal abuses or actions stemmed from government actions or encouragement.

The conservative media continued its campaign against non-Muslim religious minorities, begun after President Ahmadinejad took office in August 2005. Political and religious leaders continued to issue a stream of inflammatory statements against non-Muslims. These campaigns contributed to a significantly poorer situation for the non-Muslim community throughout the year.

Unknown actors desecrated Bahai graveyards in a number of cities. The government did not seek to identify or punish the perpetrators. Throughout the year, Bahais in several cities were targets of arson attacks; in all cases, police said nothing could be done to find the perpetrators. Some arson cases appeared to be linked to Bahai interactions with members of other religious groups, as letters were sent to owners of burned businesses shortly after the fires warning Bahais not to befriend Muslims.

There were reported problems for Bahais at different levels of society around the country. Bahais experienced continued personal harassment, including receiving threatening notes, compact discs, text messages, and tracts. There were reported cases of Bahai children being harassed in school and subjected to Islamic indoctrination. Students and educators especially targeted Bahai girls in an attempt to create sectarian tensions between parents and children.

There were numerous reports of Shia clerics and prayer leaders denouncing Sufism and the activities of Sufis in the country in both sermons and public statements.

Anti-Semitism remained a problem. Many Jews sought to limit their contact with or support for the state of Israel due to fear of reprisal. Anti-American and anti-Israeli demonstrations included the denunciation of Jews, in contrast to the past practice of denouncing only "Israel" and "Zionism." In November, a Jewish woman in Isfahan was reportedly stabbed to death and her body was mutilated during a land dispute. Her family members had been receiving threats as they pursued legal action to claim back part of their house that had been expropriated and attached to a neighboring mosque. The family could not definitively state the crime was religiously motivated.

There were reports during the year that members of the Sabean-Mandaean community experienced societal discrimination and pressure to convert to Islam.

Section IV. U.S. Government Policy

Since 1999 the United States has designated Iran as a "Country of Particular Concern" (CPC) under the International Religious Freedom Act for having engaged in or tolerated particularly severe violations of religious freedom. In August 2011 the secretary of state redesignated Iran as a CPC, and redesignated the existing restrictions on certain imports from and exports to the country, in accordance with section 103(b) of the Comprehensive Iran Sanctions Accountability and Divestment Act of 2010, pursuant to section 402(c)(5) of the act.

The United States has no diplomatic relations with Iran, and thus did not directly raise concerns with the government over its religious freedom abuses and restrictions. However, the U.S. government made its position clear through public statements and reports, support for relevant UN and NGO efforts, diplomatic initiatives, and sanctions as it pressed for an end to government abuses. On numerous occasions U.S.

government officials, including the ambassador at large for international religious freedom, addressed the situations of Bahai, Christian, Jewish, and other communities in the country.

In February the Departments of State and Treasury imposed sanctions against the Ministry of Intelligence and Security for being responsible for or complicit in the commission of serious human rights abuses against the Iranian people. The ministry was designated in part for its arrests and detention of members of the Bahai community without charges.

On several occasions throughout the year, the Department of State criticized the detention of citizens solely for expressing political beliefs. For example, in February and July, the Department condemned the conviction of Pastor Youcef Nadarkhani and called for his immediate release. Department officials condemned First Vice President Mohammad Reza Rahimi's anti-Semitic remarks at an international conference on drug abuse in June.

In March the United States voted at the UN Human Right Council to renew the mandate of the UN Special Rapporteur for human rights in Iran. The United States also voted in November at the UN Third Committee in favor of a resolution expressing concern over Iran's human rights practices, including the increased persecution of religious minorities.